Forever Eighty-Eights

FOREVER EIGHTY-EIGHTS

POEMS BY

Molly Rice

Press 53
Winston-Salem

Press 53, LLC
PO Box 30314
Winston-Salem, NC 27130

First Edition

Cover art, "Equinunk, Route 191," Copyright © 2021
by Grant Haffner.
Used by permission of the artist.

Author photo by Jackson Shoe

Library of Congress Control Number
2022946558

ISBN 978-1-950413-54-6

In memory of

Mary Lou, Harold, Fred, Mike, Debbie, Wayne, Molly Ruth

and dedicated to

Michelle Fitzpatrick
Adrian & Micah Rice

Romans 8:18

Acknowledgments

Grateful acknowledgments are due to the following sources for previous hospitality to some of these poems: *Poetry Super Highway*; *Fortnight Magazine*; *The Stinging Fly*; *A Conversation Piece—Poetry and Art* edited by Adrian Rice and Angela Reid (Ulster Museum, Northern Ireland); *The Best of Poetry Hickory* edited by Scott Owens; *Voices and Vision—A Collection of Writing By and About Empowered Women*; *The Best of Final Friday Reading Series* edited by Scott Douglas; Finishing Line Press, *Mill Hill*; *The Dead Mule School of Southern Literature*; *Iodine Poetry Journal*; *Bloodshot Journal of Contemporary Culture*; *FourXFour—Poetry NI*; Winston-Salem Writers' "Poetry in Plain Sight"; *Wordplay* with Jeff Davis (Asheville FM); Hickory Playground's "Quarantine Diaries"; Kai Coggin's "Wednesday Night Poetry"; and The North Carolina Poetry Society & the Weymouth Center Writers-in-Residence Reading Series.

The author would also like to gratefully acknowledge the support of the following: my family and friends, here and in Ireland, Ron Rash, (the late) Kathryn Stripling Byer, Tim Peeler, Libby Bernardin, Bud Caywood, Kai Coggin, Colin Dardis & Geraldine Dardis O'Kane, Keith Flynn, Laura Hope-Gill, Helen Losse, Scott Owens, Glenis Redmond, Jonathan K. Rice, Matthew Rice, Joan & Kate Newmann, Leslie Rupracht, Robert Canipe, (the late) Ellie Depew, Donna & Jimmy Brim, Ellen Jenkins Brown, Nancy Dagley, Joel Friedman, Virginia McKinley (and staff of Malaprops Bookstore, Asheville), Alan & Carrie Mearns, Chrisanne & Lamar Mitchell, Betty & John Orr, Lois Palmer & Shandi Ghee, Anne Rawson, Sacha (The late Duchess of Abercorn), Mike & Sandy Stevenson, Woodrow Trathen & Dorothy Maguire, Rachel Lucas, my best friend & mother-in-law Jean "Jenny" McClean, my beautiful step children Matthew Rice, Charlotte Rice, Charis Rice Clements, son-in-law Pip Clements and grandson Ray Clements, Cathy Helland Watson, and especially Kevin Morgan Watson at Press 53. And last, but by no means least, my soul mate, poet Adrian Rice—without him and my son, Micah Wayne Freeman Rice, all the clocks would stop.

Contents

*88: Amateur radio's shorthand
and CB lingo for love &
kisses; math's untouchable,
palindromic, mirrored, four-
way number; radium's atomic
number; the sky's number of
constellations; days it takes
Mercury to complete its orbit;
Chinese text message bye
bye & good fortune; Bingo's
call—2 fat ladies; black &
whites is one nickname for the
piano and 88s is another; the
speed it takes to get back to
the future; hip hop = 8th letter
of alphabet = HH = 88; dead
man's hand in poker—aces and
8s; a German gun; Interstate
88; brush-footed butterflies in
two genera—wing-stamped;
the Navy's slang for "what";
Morse code—the love heart
emoji of 1879. But not a Nazi
salute. I take back the 8 and
the 8—HH. No heiling Hitler.
Dismantle hate. Only forever
love is eighty-eights. XOXO*

White Christmas

Behind the gutted trailer,
I rode my new bike,
Stopped at the sight of strewn trash.
I kicked my kickstand into the soft grass.

Potholders, pots and pans,
Pencils, receipts, telephone bills
And red Christmas garland torn in half.

A kitchen drawer, upside down.

I moved it to sit on to save my jeans
From the wet red mud.
I booted something under my feet,
Lifted it, and then sat.

A black Santa
Painted on plywood
With a hole and a bit of string.

First thought:
He's just covered in coal—
Soot from the chimney.

But then it rang through me
Like Presbyterian bells—

Blacks have their Santa, too.
And just like their God
He is black
But always painted pale.

And I stood wanting to give Christmas
And all my whiteness back.

The Devil's Beating His Wife

God's sprinkler
set to several speeds

of run-and-hide-under-trees,
head-down-drip-from-hair,
or mouth-wide-droplet-capture

was the poor kids'
summer sweet treat,

a mud-puddle
merriment,

a high time
in the sharp cracks
of hardship.

Homefront

My mother
Rips the glow
From the lightning bug
And paints our faces
With her fluorescent fingers.

We wait and watch
With round eyes,
E l e c t r i f i e d,
For our marks—
Cheeks puffed,
Breath bated.

Crickets' cantos
Ricochet off trees.

Rough, yarn-worn fingers
Press my face.
One stripe
Down each cheek—
Warm gut glow.

All the mill hill houses
White and straight in a row
Know:

Within their walls
Wars are growing.

But tonight, with him not home,
We three little Indians
Escape a scalping
And dance in the dusk
Glowing.

Lightning Bug Lamp

Frenzied race
Me in the lead
Little stars in my jar.

Even pushed her down
To get the other she was after.

Then mommy whistled.
The race was over.

I counted the lightning bugs
In my Mt. Olive dill pickle jar.

Sixteen.
The others—well below.

I slept with my prize
On the windowsill.

I awoke and saw them
Pushing each other down
To get to the lid.

Frenzied race
All lit up—

Horrible glow
In my lightning bug lamp,
Horrible heat in my heart.

Sightings

On the hill,
In our yard
With the dogs
Under our arms.

On our backs
Full of laughs
Charlie Chips
Shoved in our mouths—
Searching for
The Big Dipper.

You said you saw it—there!
Spitting sparks
Of Charlie Chips into the air
But I never saw it.

Twinkle, twinkle
Thought I saw the Little Dipper
But was wrong.

In the dawn
We woke up
Covering our eyes
From the brightness
Of a Hallelujah sky.

♦

Follow the Drinking Gourd,
Jump the branches
Run the blue-ribbon run
Slave no more
Slave to this world no more.

Winded

Shoe-skating on top
Of the ice-covered
School storage shack

Swathed in grandmother's
Early Christmas presents—
Red fancy snowsuits with
Silver racing stripes.

My brother and I played
A game of spin, against my will.
I begged and cried and shouted
That I would tell.

He grabbed me by the belt
And pulled me round and round.
I fear-laughed as my shoes slid over the ice.

Then it happened, slick as sleet,
The belt snapped like a frozen twig.
Over the edge, legs flying, searching for a landing,
Then *smack*—
The kiss of the frozen ground.

I felt for the first time
My breath knocked
Clear out of me
Like my soul leaving my body.
The clean white ghost
Unzipping my red snowsuit and floating out.

And him up there, laughing down, then bolting.

Unable to breathe any words,
All still ice in my mouth
To tell him stop and stay
To come back.

The Silver Blade

On Church Street, after washing the last
of the supper's dishes, before turning
off the night's light, I looked out the back door's
window—in our shared lot, a parked church bus.
In sleep, I replayed the scene,
but this time, when studying the seats,
a shadow-shape took form, morphing
into a man made of darkness.
He slow motioned towards me,

in his hand a silver blade spark-flashed
a strange reaction—tranced, I opened the door
and fast-forwarded half-way to him.
Are you going to kill me?
After I kill your neighbors first.
He walked away.
Jolt-awake, I woke the house.
My mother called the neighbors—

Y'all OK?

Tired Child

after Louis le Brocquy

Pinwheel spins
As his hot breath blows
I, like a baby,
Can do nothing but gasp

Merry-go-round turns
As his hard arm throws
I, just a child,
Can do nothing but grasp

I cannot breathe
He will not stop
You laugh
You laugh

Swing

She holds the ropes tightly
Her pale pudgy body adorned in
Lavender and pink

She bends her knees and kicks air
Swinging as high as she can

Her sundress opening to the wind

Innocence

She doesn't know
He stands below
Arms crossed,
Watching.

Show Me Yours

In the woods
Shielded by the birches
We made him take down
His britches.
She stuck him with a stick
And we wondered why
He was a he and
We—a she.

Child's play
Soon found out.

Her mother hollered &
Held her by the wrist
And beat her in circles
With a bare hazel switch.
A usual spanking dance,
A sad Ring o' Roses,
And when she lost her step & fell
Her pockets were full of empty.

The Other Way

for April Renee Causby (1972-2003)

Looks like it's over, you knew I couldn't stay.

I wanted to see you again. Go back to our Mill Hill.
See ourselves swinging on our rope swing.
Remember the time it snapped mid-air and landed
Us both out of breath?
We thought that was the closest we could get to death.

We had a good thing. I'll miss your sweet love.

Mommy played the Robert John record over and over,
Directed us in a tryst.
Wayne the lover, you the wife, me the mistress—
I rehearsed my fake tears when he sang
"Sad Eyes" and you stood there
Knowing you had won,
One hand on your hip,
The other poofing your hair.
The wife he couldn't leave.

Try to remember the magic that we shared.
In time your broken heart will mend.

We moved from McAdenville.
Us first, then you.
I went to college; you dropped out of high school.
Then I didn't know where you had gone.
I searched and found you once—
Doped up and living with your dad.
You were angry with me. Said it was easy for me.
I lost you again until
I heard you had a headache,
Took pain pills and never woke up.

But it's over.
Sad eyes turn the other way.
I don't wanna see you cry.
Sad eyes, you knew there'd come a day
When we would have to say goodbye.

Girls Only

for Shell

We struck one—nothing.
We struck two and something—
Little pyro-poof!
Our hands huddled around it,
Wishing it.
We threw it down
On our dry-leaf mound
And magic!

We had a secret.
Girls only—
Since we weren't allowed in the boy's den.
But out of our hands, it went wild
And our secret
Smoke-signaled
Above the trees
Tattle-telling.

Shell-shocked we rushed
To a plastic pool
And wrestled the water
Into the woods
But it slipped from our fingers
And fell short of help.
By the time we reached
A pail of rainwater, it was way too late.

We ran home red-handed
And phoned without giving our names.
The sirens came.
The shame lasted as long as
The charred circle remained.

First from our fingers,
Then out of our hands—
Let us learn:
Not too quick to prove.
Our power is within.

Free Will

We went because our friends did.
We placed & glued our colored macaroni to make the shape
Of Jesus's face just like the rest of them.
We carefully tied our cloves in cloth
With the given ribbon.
We loved the Old Testament stories and sang
The hymns, just like the rest of them, but louder and prouder
And with our souls.
"Jesus loves me, this I know, for the Bible tells me so."

We went because our friends did
And when the whole congregation met in the main hall to feed,
We waited last in line with our paper plates for a few crumbs—
Potato chips, brownies, or chocolate cupcakes.
Like sheep we sat in the back (eyes downcast).
During the Lord's Prayer
I didn't shut my eyes.
I saw the sisters staring at us.

When the prayer was over in that last quiet moment
All heard a sister say, "Those girls only come for the food!"
And I stood, took my little sister by the hand and led her
Through the hall, walked out the front doors
And all the way home.
"Little ones to Him belong, they are weak, but He is strong."

Reduced Gravity, 1976

for Sir Patrick Moore

Pluto passing
Behind Jupiter
Left four squares
Empty,
Swings rocking
In the children's wake,
Jump ropes
In the slack position,
"Miss Mary Mack Mack Mack"
Quieted
As elementary
School-children
And teachers alike
Gravitate toward the black pavement.

Now, jump in the air
And feel the slight
Floating sensation—

Over and over
Reach for the sky

Hover

Over

Hell

And refuse
To fall in.

Childhood Memory

for Sue Hardy

I take you back—
Sometimes you close your eyes,
Other times you stare into the distance,
A smile breaks on your face.

Truth be told,
I'm painted sketchy,
Snippets of here-there/who/me-you.
Moments. Scenes of things. Exaggerated.
Stories told and re-told.
I'm stored in your brain's corridors.
The proof of my Zen
My fade in-out, out-in,
Are your keepsakes.
Those forget-me-nots
That set me going,
That pushes my play button. . .

Letters, clothes, old baby shoes, jewelry, furniture, dolls,
Photos, a poem, a scent, a place, a voice, a song. . .
The elementary drawing in your drawer
Of the house with chimney and smoke-squiggle,
Square windows crossed,
The spring seasoned tree with knot, forever green,
And the sky with bird V, cloud-puff,
And a smiling sun with rays of many shades. . .
That fridge art "for mommy on your special day"
Can take you back to you—
When you were then.

Hold me dear.
In the end, I'm all you've got.
My rewind will leave you blurry-eyed and longing for
The days that seem so far away

And will never come back.

Golden Orb Weaver

I'll whisper your name
In its web
And the writing spider
Will spin the letters
With its legs.

Always told
Never smile
Near its gilded silver-face
Hide your teeth or they'll be counted
And rot out of your head.

Black and yellow blur, inkblot belly
Rorscahach's *what might this be?*
Hand cupped over my mouth
When I saw the makings of "M"

Slow motion
Ouija board
Zigzagging Death
To your door.

Picked up a stick
And waved it like
A wand in the web
Erasing the
Start of a spell

Prayers that night
Under my canopied bed
That the spider's thread
Would not lower it
To my head

Slumbering dreams had it orb-like
Weaving its way down the canal of my ear
Chanting my name to the sound
Of an angry drum.

Pet

I found a pet, I once thought.
I put it in a box.
I fed it scraps from the table.
It scooted from one corner to the other.

I went to bed that night
thinking I had made a friend.
The next morning
I nudged it and gave it a fresh strawberry—

It was dead.

What do the tamed know?

Dogwood

The bare bark bones
They know
Up
And
Out
They know
Cold
And
Wet
And
Dark.
They know
The saw
And
How to fall.

And
Yet
They
Still
Branch

Their

Flowering

Fingers

To

God.

Forebears

Before me,
They hurt.
They lost.
They wept.

They brought forth others
To do the same.

That sunken ship,
Decades of drowned lives
That I descend into,
Dive-lighting the conjured watery world
To glimpse them in their living rooms.

A guitar strummed.
A table set.
A fire lit.
A tale told.

I want to know you but I'm only a deep diver.
Bubbles in the bone. Rapture of the deep.
Forty-five
Minutes
Then up for air—

Ascend
Pause.

Ascend
Pause.

Decompression
From death's kingdom
Bears a depression
And a longing
To go home.

Testimony

for my great grandmother Ada Chambers Fuller

On the viola the Chuck Wagon Gang
Sang "Blessed Assurance"
Tight harmonies rang true
With street corner preaching.
She saw a vision of herself burning in Hell
With a peg leg. God spoke to her and said to
Send for Preacher Martin. He slipped in through the backdoor
So not to disturb the quiet Baptist meeting
Held in the sitting room.
Her crippled leg was drawn underneath her.
He laid his hands on her and she was healed.
She walked to witness on the street corner.
She held the Bible open in one hand
Blind and illiterate she could not know the words to speak—

"Jesus will write them on the tables of your heart."
And she stood the Spirit speaking through her
Word for word God's message.
Those who knew her would marvel
And read along.

Evicted from the Judson mill hill when
She was told not to preach anymore from her porch,

She opened her windows
And shouted from inside
Raising the roof to the Holy clouds.
"No *man* will tell God what to do."
And they moved down the way
To Monaghan Mill
Where they saw no harm
In a Holiness woman.

Fuller's Flying Circus

for Ansel, Eula, Molly Ruth & Mary Lou

She said
He would
Tie a bit of string
Around a June bug
And fly it like a careworn kite.

Around
In circles
And zigzags
For the mill hill kids.
Shouting, singing, buzzing

Parading their catch
In a flea circus attempt
To humiliate and cheer the
Man-controlled creepy-crawly.

Finally
It would break
The line and fly free-willed
Higher than tiptoes and fingertips.

Fuller would
Then chase & catch another
With his pied piper antics. The children
Would crowd and audition sticky legs & tiny wings
For their next hair-raising, death-defying, amazing flying finale—
Tied to his tongue.

To Be a Boy

for Mary Lou Ellen "Virginia Ragtime Cowboy Joe"

Twisting & turning reaching & pulling
From the left one to the right one
Trying hard to kiss my elbow.

My grandmother was told if you
Could kiss your elbow you would
Magically turn into a boy.
She twisted & turned and held her mouth just right
And ran off faster, climbed a tree, rode her bike
But only to find herself still a girl—
Just a tomboy.

Twisting—
No more tears, no more makeup,
No more legs, armpits & bikini line to shave.
No more eyebrows to pluck.
No more "You're not strong enough."
No more fine lines to walk—gracefully.

Turning—
No more hurt feelings.
No more "I'm too fat." "I'm ugly." "I hate me."
No more "My breasts are too small."
No more Wonderbras, waterbras, padded bras
Or in my grandmother's days—socks in the bra.

Reaching—
No more dieting. No more starving, bingeing, purging.
No more "Eat slowly with your mouth closed."
No more "speak quietly & politely."
No more "sit up straight."
No more polishing, primping, pruning & prancing.

Pulling—
No more burden of baby bringing pain.
No more hormonal hell of the change of life.

Lies—
No more princesses & knights in shining armor,
Big ball gowns draped & shimmering on you and your beauty.

Fear—
No more locking the door, double-locking the door,
"Did I lock the door?" Better put a chair under the doorknob.

No more
Put downs,
Stand on's,
Brush offs,
Push arounds.

No more smile, keep smiling,
Put Vaseline on your teeth to keep smiling.
Still wondering will I be in last place?

No more.

I want to kiss my elbow.
To be a boy, a man, Zeus.
To not be told what to do and how to do it.
To be strong, to be accepted,
To drop the shell and pick up the sword.

But it is impossible to kiss my elbow
(And the boys always knew it)
Impossible to be top dog—
(And settling for tomboy is doubly cruel)
So I'll get my bobbin and my yarn
And make me a boy and train him well.

Raising Cain

It's not easy raising Cain.
He's quite a handful.
Always kicking & biting—
Throwing his weight around—
Not like his brother.

It is not easy raising Cain.
He loves to raise Hell.
Always pitching a fit.
He sasses & cusses & spits.
And would as soon cut ya as look at ya.
The spitting image of
His daddy—the bullying bastard.
Nothing like his brother.
Or his mother.

Tough Love

I'll jerk a knot in your ass.
I'll knock you clear into next week.
I'll box your jaws.
I'll wipe that smirk right off your face.
I'll knock your head off.
I'll beat the Hell out of you.
I'll kill ya and swear you died.
I'll backhand you.
I'll knock your teeth down your throat.
I'll shake the shit out of you.
I'll smack you so hard it will make your head spin.
I'll give you something to cry about.
Don't back talk me!
Don't you give me that look!
Get out of my sight.

Lullaby

Say it again,
"A mistake"

Banned to my bedroom at night
Between *Hogan's Heroes* & *Good Times*

"A Mistake"

You are, little one,
A mistake.

Hickory Switches

I'd slam the screen door
On my way out
To pick my own punishment stick.

"And you'd better bring in a big one!"
So I searched for the switch that wasn't too big
But one that would satisfy her.

Looking through the bush
Beside my bedroom window,
I found one.
I broke off the branch
And stripped it bare—
Leaving only one leaf for luck.

A switchin' for a lie or a sass
That would leave my bare legs stingin'
And sometimes if she was real pissed off
Leave them bleedin'.

Sir, No Sir

I scratched and sparked
"I hate the devil."
With a bit of flint right on the spot
Where you parked your beat-up pickup.
It took time going over the letters again and again.
Bold for the first time.

I whispered
"Rebuke" and then "Bind Satan"
When I saw you pass the church
And fly down the hill.

I hid—scared of your flared nostrils, your flicked cigarette,
Your steel-toed boots. You got out of the truck
And flung the door shut.
I dropped my rock and flinched.
I watched your hurried hunchback gait cross the yard
And then the slam of the screen door.

You didn't even take notice of my work.

I was ready to lie
If you held me by the scruff, lifting me off the floor,
Threatening to knock my teeth down my throat.
I would have said,
"No, no, not you, Daddy, the devil, not you, sir."

Christmas Town, USA

Under these lights,
Magic can happen.
Even Satan can turn into Santa.

His beard—not a tangled forest of shadow.
His boots—not kicking your ribs.
His belt with golden buckle not marking your body.
His suit—not a uniform marching to the boilers.
His "ho, ho, ho"—not a yelling curse.

Under these lights,
(450,000 red, white and green flame)
There is a glimmer of a smile.
Some warmth.

Pawn shop presents are not ticking time bombs.
Dogs are not hiding under the couch.
Singing is not told to shut up.
We are not made to eat in the kitchen alone.
Flinching is nowhere to be found.

But the moon hangs over us
And the blinking lights fade
Fear enters noisily caroling
That Christmas comes
Only once a year.

McAdenville

Rewind the time:
Elementary school plays with "It's a Small World" theme, field day ribbons
kept in Bibles, monkey bars, times tables, *The Electric Company*, taking
off my shoes walking to & from school

The streets paved for Big Wheels, bikes, Lemon Twists, and roller skates,
speed bumps that didn't slow us down

Neighbors' houses, yards and all, were your own, welcomed to come and
go at our own free will

Up and down the town plenty of hills on our Mill Hill

Living at the bottom of Church Street above the trailer park, Lakeview
Baptist was in our yard
nooks of time-spending outside the church walls,
Barbie doll dance hall

Digging for earthworms and grubs, dirt in the Duke's Mayonnaise jar,
Roly-polys little bug ball, hoping to find a Garter snake

Magnolia trees the blossoms and the seed pods all toys to me—
weapons with red seeds

Crape Myrtle buds flowerpockets pushed out before their time to see
pink or white bloom

Walking everywhere you go, the whole town a family that you
know—a village

The dead man's curve makes you feel like for a split-second you will
crash into the lake head-first and drown

The big house on the hill overlooking the lake everybody's dream house—
far-fetched—it's always the case of "all sewn up"

Fire station and police department in the heart of the town never heard a tale but knew they were ready to spin on a dime

The "Little Rainbow" fishing for crawdads and minnows, careful not to cut your foot wide-open on broken beer bottles

Fishing under the mill not catching a thing, the lake lit-up or not a fountain forever flowing, trees all around, in a row ducks crossing the wee bridge

Horrible monster noise when opening the mill's doors beware of the textile teeth

The Village Inn restaurant where pancakes were free when we would sit at their counter and say that we were as hungry as all get out

Downtown—a post office, a tiny grocery store, newspaper boxes, a pay phone, the town clock slipping time into the future

Swim team stars and stripes suits, backstroke, breaststroke, swimming pool, night swim, diving board, lifeguards, wet prune fingers dabbing at the crumbs of sour cream and onion potato chips and chugged full of red Hawaiian Punch, summer's sidewalk burns even if it's wet

Community Center after school, bumper pool, basketball, buddies

Jr. Midgets and Pee Wees, cheerleading practice, football nights, hot chocolate to warm freezing hands—The orange and blue McAdenville Dolphins couldn't be beat, we're #1, "Firecracker firecracker boom boom boom"

Fourth of July fireworks at the baseball field, blankets, lawn chairs, grass that wanted wear, shorts and tube tops

Mr. Pharr's mansion—maids at the door, Easter egg hunt, golden egg prize, grandfather figure with love in his eyes

Halloween jack-o'-lanterns carved for baking pumpkin seeds, costumes homemade, haunted house at the church, crawling through cardboard, hands grabbing your hair, reach into mystery box, peeled grapes for eyeballs

Aviary Gardens our own small zoo, bird show plume, peacocks, glory feathers that we didn't know shouldn't be brought into your home, evil eye, bad luck, llama spit, monkey business

Christmas town, USA—prizes for the best door decoration, proud mother third place, town all a-glow, cars come and go slowly very slowly, the lake in its best light

South Fork River Bridge crossing fear, my brother daredeviled the rails over red mud banks to the convenient store for glass bottles of Coke, pour in salted peanuts and watch it fizz

McAdenville Lake Dam—always holding back but sometimes flying off the handle taking a life or two

The yarn mills—inside a hive of lost parents—outside kids latch-keyed—the village raised their young.

Fast forward to today:
Condos constructed where the mill hill once sang sweet Southern story—a cat's cradle whose strings will never fray.

Pharr Yarns

Who is left?
Who will do the millwork?

I have carried this millstone
Without complaint
Without contempt
And I have breathed the dirt and lint
Like my parents did before me.
And their parents did before them.
And theirs before them.

I have spliced till palsy comes
And my canteen coffee spilt

The baby in my belly
Resembles me not.
The Mill Hill is razed

And now
Ghosts out

Across the threadbare distance.

T

Terminate.
Tear down.
Take away.
Torch.

The blue spray-painted "T"
Marks the mill hill houses
For extinction.

Nothing's left
Even the memories
Are tagged by time.

It's no use trying to save them.
The mills are going-going-gone.
Money, money, money
The machines are coming.

Muscle-out.
Move over.
Make way.

For what's next.

Hurt

Sticks & stones
May break my bones
But those words
They haunt me.
Haunt me.
Haunt
Me.

Clipping for Quarters

for John Gladden and his trailer park

Old Man Gladden
Came for me on his blue tractor.
He'd pull up in the yard
And I'd get my things—
Pocket knife and silver clippers.

I dug out the dirt,
Dirt from the turnip-green fields,
Dirt from his plow and potted plants,
Dirt that he couldn't get out.
Dirt that waited for me.

I pushed the dull pocket knife
Back into its shell.

Then, the silver clippers.
I'd cut his nails—
Worrying not to cut into the quick
Of his old quaking fingers,
Careful as a little girl could be.
My pink-as-pigs fingers shaking, too.

I'd finish and give him a smile.
He'd carry on for a while
On the porch with my grandparents,
Sitting a spell.

As he'd stand to go,
He'd reach into his denim overalls
For my "fee."

A quarter for digging out the dirt,
A quarter for his clean clipped nails.

Thou Shalt Not

In the summer she wore culottes.
She wasn't allowed to show skin in shorts.

She couldn't slip on a swimsuit
so they wouldn't let her in

at *Suttle's Mudpuddle*
my favorite swimming spot.

She couldn't cut her hair
so she wore it tight in a bun.

Mrs. Tucker would yell after her
to call her in

when we were picking teams
for a little trailer park kickball.

She couldn't run around and get too hot
because she was Southern Fundamental Baptist

And being born a girl
there's a lot of thou-shalt-nots.

Knocker-upper

She was a pro knocker-upper.
She'd tap three times on the single wide
under my bedroom window.

I'd feign awakeness and knock back.
But fall back to sleep not wanting to be present
in the schoolfactory.

She'd do her rounds, come in,
cook, and bring me breakfast
on a tin Smurf tray.

Eggs, bacon, hash browns,
grits or oatmeal
and blossoms from the yard.

She was the reason I was awake.
She was the reason
I was awake at all.

She selflessly
gave me morning. A real
ray for the rest of my days.

Many Moons Ago

for Glenis Redmond

Rusty mudshoes
cracking,
dorsums decorated
with hematite,
made where I believed
Satan swayed
to make
desiccation.
Him coming up
from hell
to our soles, for our souls.
A summer time-spender—
who could last the distance
in the boulder boots?
Mars-mud red,
we moved
elephant-
heavy—
elephant-
slow—
back to the trailer
transformed with
outer-space-slow-mo.
Grandmother
met us at the ramp
with a hose
Y'all dirty
And ain't coming no closer!
All we packed in from our mission
lost in the quick orbit of water.

Hereafter

after Langston Hughes

It's had shouting in it,
And slapping,
And yanking hair,
And places you can't hide your
Fear.

You turned your cheek and finally
Set down on the steps
And smoked deeper
Eyes fixed on what could have been.
No, no crystal stair here
Despair
And lucky you are now
Elsewhere.

Real Sex

I

Walking home from school,
We found the pack of pills—
Some strange circular Pez.
We looked to my brother
Because he was the oldest.
Birth Control.
I kicked it with my sneaker
To flip it over.
We stared
Wondering if we touched
It with our fingers
Would we turn into sex?

II

On the drive-thru window's ledge
I saw it while preparing the day's shift.
I called Cora over
Because she was the oldest.
She giggled—a French Tickler.
A right monster's mask.
A red rubber used and slung out.
I picked it up with a stick
Put it in a to-go bag, double-tied it
And threw it out with the trash.
I hoped he loved her
And not just the sex.

First Date

I knew he didn't allow
Sitting in the car after a date,
But we were listening
To "Every Rose Has Its Thorn."

He high-stepped
Up the yard
Fuming.

By the time I noticed,
He had nearly ripped
The car door off its hinges
And pulled me out by my hair.

Half way down, dragging me
Through the yard,
He lifted me up enough
To punch me in the face.

All in front of the boy
Who reversed as quick as he could
To get out of the hellhole
And no longer be witness.

In the house, he slut-shamed me.
You are nothing
But a licked lollipop!

Weeping, I tried to explain,
But to shun further fists to my face
I went to my room and called
The guy one last time

And said between gullies of sobs
It's over.

Stray

Before the school bus
In my good school clothes—
I fished out the drowned stray cat
With a long pole net
Black and belly bloated
Heavy as all get out

I strained and sweated
And got all wet
The bus went by
And beeped its horn
I knew I had
A few minutes more
He'd have to turn around
On the dead-end road

I muscled and fought
To drag that cat
From the green slimy pond of a pool
But had to leave her buoyant

On the bus
Everyone loud and carrying on
But I sat
With the cat away with my tongue
Taking it with her
Beyond death
In her bulging black sack.

The Hot Hole

The river rats knock back Coors in a can all night.
They rack up their empties and pyramid them
On the red mud bank like a shrine
To their lost opportunities.
They fish, they fight, they forgive.
They get wild and swim out too far.

When they crawl into their tent
And pass out at dawn,
I creep over and watch the wriggling
Stringers full of crappie, bass, and catfish.

Each one a trapped kin.
A collection of their strung sins
That I baptize, unthread mouths and gills
—Submerge—
Saving them from the knife.
A second birth.
My parents' power plant's prize released
Releases a deluge of fear.
A price to pay.

Jukebox Gold

Bar-hopping legend.
You could shove a cue ball
into your mouth and spit it in the side pocket
without a shadow of a doubt.
A bar box hustle
you pretended suited you just fine.
But I know there was a
woman trapped inside
shaking the bars
who would have much rathered
a conversation about the cosmos,
a shake, rattle and roll in the jukebox gold
much rathered a song from the soul
not the country twang
of where you landed.
Not the *love the one you're with*
but a holy union where Jesus dwelt
and not a drunk man's hands
fiddling your thighs.
Quiet eyes.
Bad break.

Your side pocket
scratch
left you losing out
as the jukebox
Honky-Tonked on
and on.

Hooked—
then
walking
the floor.

Dumped

He dumped me today.
No forewarning.
His black boot on my head
making me little
to squeeze me into the
blue-black Hefty trash bag.
He double-tied me
in with his leftovers
and his beer cans.

Settling in
and getting used to the smell,
I was shocked still—
freeze frames of his eyes,
his mouth, when he said
like scripture
there was somebody else.

De press i on

The Black Dog
Is at my door.

I've been feeding him scraps
Of the day—

He tries to get in my bed
At night as I lay my head down
But I kick him out by shutting my eyes.

He runs off.

I hear his distant
Bark. He'll not be back
Until I whistle
For him.

Someone else has opened
Their screen door.
He has taken abode.

The noose
Like a leash
By the door.

Let Go

The trash truck of my soul hauls a heavy load.
Each stop overflowing sin bins
Crippling the garbage man.
Each stop—a solid waste of time.
Each stop—a shake the dust.
A carry on compost.
A landfill burial
Of regret.
Of forget.
But sprouting
From the pile—
The moss of
Forgiveness.

Fried Green Tomatoes

Walking behind my mother
Through the tall wet grass—
As a child I ran through
At her heels,
Barefooted,
Taking no notice
Of what was under my feet
Or the whipping lashes
Of the grass branding my bare legs.

Now wading in the shallows
Of the thigh-high yard grass,
I think of the wet sting
And dirtying my stylish
Thirty-something retro blue
Tennis shoes.

Walking way, way behind
My mother,
Who still barefoots
& hightails the trails
And lays back the grass
Like a bushman.

She wants to show me something.

Wiping the bugs off my legs,
I reach her.
The whole time I think Calamine.
And she smiles at my faded courage
And points to her green tomato vines.

Mine

The day she stroked
words exploded
across the divide
of our households.
The slamming
of the receiver
blasted a
forever-ravine
in my heart.

It is mine.
Never to dial back—

the canary
still dead
in my
remorseful
mouth.

Boilermaker

It didn't take much
to make you fume
The still-stand
dead-in-your-tracks
welded fists
the breath
smoking like
puffs of steam
the long train
of your stare
Then through
tight teeth
the ungodly gruff
The last time
you scorched me
was on a
Christmas Eve
I'd asked too many
times about
a letter
that I was
waiting for to arrive
in your mailbox
I didn't trust your
delivery
I stood at
the sink
and
you
started
I'll knock your goddamn teeth
down your throat.

I damned back
my tears
until

the car
journey
home
They burst
out
and brought
with them
the ghosts
of all other
times you
put your words
fists feet
on all of us
You will die
old man
I will
cry then
too

Cut Short

The Jim Walter Home
rooted on the given
land from his father
stood unfinished inside.
She planted impatiens in
the front under her open
window.

She brushed her teeth
over the tub. He never got
around to fully installing
the sink. She wrote on
the bathroom sheetrock
Here I sit broken-hearted
Came to shit but only farted.
He never found the time
to complete her a home.
Work was an excuse and
drinking was the reason.

She cuddled herself lonely on the
couch. Never found the
need to dress. No
where to go except
the manufactured dreamworld
of HBO.
No real heat except
from the potbelly stove.
No AC to keep her cool.
She suffered it
and he didn't give a damn.

And after her brain attack,
he sought the bottom
of bottles and remarried
soon after.

She moved in.
A look-alike.
He didn't miss
a beat.
Then she too had a stroke
and now he's alone
the unfinished walls
closing in.

Liftings

His bed was pristine clean.
He was neatly tucked in.
The lilies the daughter brought in
Were set by the off TV—
Enough of this world—
The rattle of reality.
She spoke to him like you would a child,
That soothing loving lilt,
You have visitors.
He, heavy with cancer and meds, came to.
He spoke in slow motion.
He half-smiled.

♦

The same way my brother did
When he was Earth-bound.
But his deathbed
Was the front seat of his home,
Head on steering wheel,
Overdosing himself
Out of this stifling town.

♦

Aunt Molly's was her own bed.
Her own secret blood pooled
And seeped into the covers
But her face—a porcelain doll
Fixed and ready for rapture.

♦

My mother's—a hospital bed.
My sister dry-washed her hair

And cleaned her feet. I sang and
She touched my lips.
The massive stroke of the clock,
The constant TV company—
She slipped away—morphine mute.

♦

Now, when the phone rings
I think it is grief calling
Telling of another lifting.

Household

for Robert Mearns—Proverbs 31:10-30

And you didn't know
When you came
To visit
Bringing
Thoughtful
Gifts to
Welcome baby

That I was
Bowled under
The fear of being
Mother

You said
You were my pastor
So they'd not question
Your intent
But the Almighty
Knew your face
Would send me
Some peace.
Some words.
Some comfort.

Missing my
Own mother
Whom I was wove
In her womb
Her tomb came
Too soon to meet
My son.
So tears had come
And fears kept watch
But when you showed
God released me
And I knew that
I'd not fear for my household—
As scarlet is our garment.

Time to Time

I know how fast time goes
I watch you grow

and conjure the others from their graves
who time called too soon

in mosaic memory
piecing together their
hands
smiles
words
eyes
hugs

Moments
Monumental
mementos

Each a tessera that builds
for the time being
landscapes
that I make into
my dreamscape

Tucking you in at night we always say
Where are we going to meet?
Lucid scenes to deny our sleep separation
a field of daisies
a floating cloud
back in Ireland
by the Shimna playing
with Ray
All our happy places
And you keep growing
and I keep withering

In good time
I hope to see them again pieced back together
in all their glory and these words bring you
my son
the same solace

Spaced Out

At the gate of here & elsewhere
You drift beyond my reach.
Are you spaced out, son?
Hello, Earth to Micah, come in, Micah.
You slight-smile but you're still stunned slow.

Decoupled from here
The gate wide open—
You run through zones
A mental free verse
An offline mode
The fields of thought
Crossing constellations
You catch your wandering mind
In the net of now
Close the gate & say

What?

Brief

for C.K. Williams

After the news
on the newsfeed was said—
that the poet at 78 was dead,
a sad silence
fell about our heads
except for the
five-year-old.

He has no time for grief.
There is jumping
and laughter to be had.
There is no shushing
his need for the now.
No brief moment for
the long train of grief.

He cups his hands
and shouts
down the pathway through pain
his voice echoing precociously—
Play!

By Hand

I help grandmother now
Wash her dishes.
She would never go to bed
With a sink-full.
Seems like the dishes never end.

When I was
A girl it was my job
And with a family of five
They pile up
If you don't keep at them.

By hand—glasses first.
Put in the silverware to sink
And soak.
Plates lining up in the rack,
Bowls on top,
Or anywhere you can angle them.

Pots and pans were the worst,
Greasy or stuck sauces,
And of course last to be dealt with.

I'd squeeze the *Joy*
And would wish on the bubbles.
If there were any,
It would be a good day.

I'd drift on daydream while I washed
Or quietly sulk in secret,
Luckily my back was to
The house facing a
Window to nowhere.

At times, I'd focus on the job
At hand

And pretend I was in a cleaning contest.

Once she heard me accidently drop
A dish, she rushed in
And saw the dish broken on the floor.
She slapped my face so hard
My grandchildren felt it.
I cried all night
When she claimed I broke
It on purpose so I wouldn't have to wash it.

She later came to my bedside
And said she was sorry to have
Hit me and that she loved
Her grandmother.

The one that was blind
That colored her dog purple
And she didn't have the heart to say
To her it wasn't brown when she asked.
The one who loved Jesus
And took her to get grilled cheese
On the trolley.
That plate was all she had left.

Before she died, and he died,
My brother and I
Stood at her sink
He washed, I rinsed.
Him elsewhere.
Me babbling on
Not knowing
It was our last moment.

Now, my husband does
The washing up in our house.
He does them in his own manner
With his mind a million miles away.

DYB

for Ellen Brown

My mother grabbed my coveted Christmas present—
The Panasonic shoebox portable cassette recorder—
As soon as she heard our favorite tune
Blast over the radio waves.

She'd mostly hit the red record button just
In time for the first verse.
She'd push play then pause play then pause
Until the lyrics were written down to ready us
For the McAdenville Elementary Talent Show.

She planned out our dance moves on
The yellow kitchen linoleum floor.
I practiced until I got it all right.

> Don't It Make My Brown Eyes Blue
> Upside-Down
> Best Of My Love
> You're In My Heart

Years of songs under my belt,
A teacher saw my love
Of the stage & cast me in my first
Show—a ringmaster.

The makings of my love
Of suspending disbelief.
My mother is now long gone.
I pull her close to me
As I fret for my boy tonight.

He is backstage.
It is his first time in a wee skit &
The Gymnatorium is packed-out.

Through our rehearsal times at
Cub Scouts, at school, at Ivey's house—
He tried to quit. He even
Feigned sickness on the day of.

His dad on the walk home from school,
After his teacher mentioned Micah was
Complaining of a headache, fever,
Spoke quietly and kindly and reminded
Him that a gentleman finishes
What he starts & doesn't let
His team down.

And there he is

The horrible before feeling.
His wee worried eyes
Brow bent in half
Trying to distract himself
And the others waiting.
I gave him
Tichy good luck
As I do all my
Teenage actors,
More to comfort
Myself and walked away
Back to my seat nestled
Between dad and cheering friend.

Curtains open on
Oakwood's Got Talent &
Nervously the troupe
Do their cub scout skit.

Afterwards, on our walk
To the car, he confessed
That he nearly ran off stage.
He said he wanted to run away
And never stop running.

Where I relish the spotlight,
He does not. His shyness strange to me.

I was so proud. He was able
To fight stage fright
To stay
To see it through
To finish what he started
To slay his monster-fear-list of what-ifs—
What if I mess up?
What if the audience leaves?
What if I vomit?
What if my friends mess up?
What if people make fun of us?

I was proud. He was proud.
The prize of praise
Not of being "Number One"
Not of being "THE best"
But of DYB—Do Your Best—
Whatever that best is at the moment.

To not give up
When you are up front
On the front line
Stand up even when all
Eyes are on you.
DYB DYB DYB.

Present

And so
Christmas comes quickly in,
Awkwardly sits on shelves
And tilts to the right side from the floor.

Icons of elves,
Snowflakes,
Reindeer,
The holly and the ivy.

Noel, all-aglow.

We muster good cheer for the child
As we well-know, he is of the age to remember
And we are creating his childhood memories.

We talk back of our own—the when, the how
I ask, which tradition should we start?
The presents under the tree before the day
Or the Santa story?

Full knowing that my Christmas spirit will
Be manufactured as it left with the death
Of my beloved brother and mother—
The merry-makers, the Christmas-lovers.

Even though reared in Christmastown, USA
I have no patience for this season where our
Savior is buried under mountains of wasted trees
Ironically, green and pine tree print.
And stuff piled upon stuff
That we will soon forget.

But I don't want to steal the joy
From my husband or my boy
I'll pray Christmas away
And know the real reason
Is to presently
Be.

Harvest the Wind

after "Zahra's Whirled"

They are like pinwheels,
blown by your breath,
shaped by the sun—
still innocent within.
Your whorling words
are a constant chime,
a reminder of who
they can be.
Careful
as you speak
them
into the
spinning world.
They go so fast
out of your hands
and are no longer all yours.
In childhood play,
they grow
and test
their speed.
Lead them,
teach them,
protect and love them
until they harvest the wind
and stand strong like a turbine
bringing back the very laughter
you once had
when you too
were
knee-high
to the world.

Tabled

for Tammy Cordeiro

Unopened bills,
walkie-talkies,
days-old salsa and chips,
piled-up school worksheets,
an apple—a game of send and return to sender
each day in a Fortnite book bag—
pencil shavings,
a mid-played monopoly game,
Third grade photos that need ordering,
Black Friday ads,
my grandmother's recipe for turkey dressing,
an empty Ziploc baggie,
all pushed aside to make space
for me. And
poetry.
Shy-starts.
Stuttering, spoke gently and sorried
the times I pushed her
to the backburner.
She said,
I know. I know.
And so here we are, the two of us, gathered.
Bowing our heads. Untying the untidy.
Quietly, secretly, as someone needs me somewhere.
And I know she will understand if I leave again.
But how long until next time, as years may fail me.
And they might need
my words to comfort them.
Just a few more
Before I—

Blazed

after AR

I took him to
Play pinball
To grant you
Time to
Browse books—
Your favorite
Past-time—
When suddenly
I sunk into sorrow
With the thought of
A tomorrow where
I alone would
Landmark our
Memories.

Breathless,
I was led
Back to the
Front Seat of my car
Where I
Held my breath
And slipped my hand
Into your blazer
To ask your heart
To beat with my heart
And we sat
Wordless,
Blazed
With the
Car aflame.

Braving the Waves

for Adrian

He was all buckle and lift
And leaned his shoulder in
Bracing the tackle of the wave.
It bashed and blindsided
But the only thing fazed
Were his swim trunks.
The yellow flag cautioning
From the lifeguard's perch.
The rip tide kept his face furrowed.
How his wide shoulders, soaked from his approach,
Beamed in the refereeing sun.
So many days I've sheltered there in the
Safety of those broad dunes.
His winning was knowing
At any moment any of us could lose.

Coronals

for Craig Wyant

I.
Don't pull the flowers
Leave them for the bees
But find
Wee treasures
For us to gather
And make a wreath
And lay it on the grave
Of defeat
And brighten a Roman-victory
To beat the blues—
For Christ
To come in.
Circling Wild Onion,
Patterning pebbles,
Placing a cracked-open
Black walnut,
The boy says looks like a dog's nose
Sticks, leaves, a Magnolia branch—still green,
The coveted lost marbles, now found,
Behind the bushes brings the color
And the perfect purple of Chrisanne's flowering Rosemary.
The trappings of making merriment
Through this unseen season.
What will we call it?
The boy replies, Callumbee.
I ask why.
I just like the way it sounds
Call um bee

II.
Our family dander
To the empty
Elementary.
Cut-out hearts fanfare
The windows of *We Miss You.*
We jump rope, swing, kick
A flat soccer ball and lap the tarmac track.
Ghosted children pockets full of posey.
The path back
We search-partied
The ground
For sculpture-worthy
Relics:
A broken #2 pencil;
A Welch's fruit snack pack;
A Pine Tree's cone;
Leaves; pink, white, red,
Petals from fallen flowers;
A Post-It note, penned
"For Daisy, to not forget."
The boy simply called it—
Oakwood Walk.

III.
A friend on Facebook
Likened our Coronals
To the Satin Bowerbird's
Attempt to attract his mate,
Whose eye is trinket blue.
The bending Maypole,
The thatched twigged, the hours
Of design
Assembling shells, berries, money,
Bright flowers, and any plastic thing
That he gets his beak on—
Color-coding the lawn of the bower
Just to woo.
O world,
What do we do to woo you
To shelter in place,
To quarantine,
To isolate?

Stepping Out

Stepping out he wore his hat
A real southern gentleman
Would not go without—
A decision of function
Rather than fashion
But dapper nonetheless.

My toddling son
Loved putting his caps on
They'd swallow him whole
And he would say
That boy's not growing at all

Take it off when you sit down to eat
Take it off indoors
Take it off in reverence

Take it off and rest it on a rack
When you are no longer going anywhere
But your armchair
And old age and dementia
Keep you planted like a Willow Oak tree—
A canopy over your living memories.

White Tee

In the dream I had of you
You were standing tall and young
In the trailer's kitchen
In your signature white tee with front pocket.

The ones I wore as a girl as a gown
I'd stretch them over my knees
And sit over the vented heat
Filling up the white shirt
Like a hot air balloon

Lifting me higher than the fear
Of my other home
Where I could not wear a gown
Without feeling his eyes on me.

In the dream your pocket was empty
But once held your brand of nicotine sin—
Chesterfield. You told me to come
To the truck with you.
When I peered out the window
I saw your dead brother in the driver's seat.
I startled awake

And knew soon you would leave me again.
The first time was when dementia
Came down the dirt road...

For now, we write *H.T. Roddy*
On the label of the big & tall v-neck
To make sure the Home
Doesn't put it on
Somebody else's
Back.

Genesis

But such a tide as moving seems asleep,
Too full for sound and foam,
When that which drew from out the boundless deep
Turns again home. —Tennyson

In my Irish scarf, I cradled his ashes
And knelt at the altar of his last wishes
To scatter among the waves
My grandfather's remains

Every inch of him—the coastline of love

The many miles he'd driven us down
Each summer
Happy enough to sit
Perched on the balcony
And watch us
His body barnacled

I told him I forever-loved him
And held him
As he once did baby-me
I thanked him for everything
Simple words
Whispered on the ocean's breeze
I dipped him under
The next gentle-lapping breaker

He slipped through my fingers
To the foam on the granular blanket of quartz, feldspar, mica
Into the skeletons of moon snails, ear shells, lightning whelk,
Banded tulip, scotch bonnet

His ashes—sand
His bones—shell

Gone.
Bygone.
Genesis.

Vacant

My heart
unfurnished
since you
went
the way
of all flesh.
I hoard
busyness
and place
you
in its steps.
My get-along
springless
since you
eighty-sixed.
my
stark heart
poor
at its very
crest.

Yours Alone

The Ring Wrestling Magazine
May 1968 featured a photo
of my grandmother in their
"Galaxy of Gal Grapplers."

The pin-up
pinned-down,
in a scissorhold
of grief, my heart
in permanent squeeze.

The rush of the find
had me searching
the roll call
of the hotbed
and how many
bouts could be had.

Two out of three falls.

The Saturday televised ringside of
the all-star eras of Flair, Rowdy Roddy Piper,
Koloff, Two Ton, Andre the Giant, Gorgeous George,
Valentine, Jake the Snake, Rip Hawk, Steamboat,
Magnum, The Fabulous Moolah, Blackjack,
Valiant, Weaver, Rich, Young, & Wahoo
to name a few.

To be without her
I'm unmasked in a squash match.
I'm on the mat in a
Figure-4 Grapevine Hold
I scream *give give*
No one hears.
Nobody knows.

When grief is yours
It is yours alone.

Redbird

(The first Christmas Eve without her)

I
The first gift to his father
Was a redbird for his desk.
At seven, he knew the bird would
Watch over him from the
Branch of his bookshelf
To fly his pen over the sky of page.
To memorialize moments.

II
We fed the redbirds
Twelve months of the year.
Most striking their fire feathers
On the white snow. Seed easy to find
A helpful handful.
She and I
Feeders of the sun & her daughter.

III
Our cardinal loss left us knowing
We have become the front line as you often remind me.
The redbird's song sent to cheer us up
Or cheer us on. Seeing one in Southern tale
Is to receive messages from loved ones who went first.
We are what's left.
The redbird sings & hinges my heart to yours.

Singer

for Kathryn Stripling Byer

Precision stitches.
Her Singer
Hummed
The thread
Zig-zagging
Reversible
Wrap-around skirts
And costumes
For my school plays.
Seemed so
Foreign to
Me when she
Showed me how
To wind the bobbin—
Afraid that I would
Break something.
The surgeon's light
Of the machine
Made it seem
So final.
Too afraid
Of the treadle
To trust
My own
Attempts.
But
By hand
I helped her
Thread the
Eye
And tie knots
And push pins into
The tomato-fashioned
Pin-cushion.
House-wifing

Seemed intimidating.
Seamstress—
Stressful.
She was a pro,
But as she put it,
Had it to do.
Her
Patterns
Forever stitched in me.
Now,
Her machine sits dusty
Faintly
Singing its rhythm of creation.

Dust to Dust

I
And they would have loved
that they made mischief on their first flight.

Is this your bag? What's in it?

My grandparents. Their ashes.

The shadow of her surgical screw—
the titanium told and radiated an alert in the scanner.
The TSA dumbfounded and embarrassed
packed the baggies back and gave them a sad pat.
I overly thanked him and quipped—

First-time flyers, internationally.

He couldn't wait to see the back of me.

II
After a double-shift one day, I bought
the gift shop kitsch "Ashes of Old Lovers"
she pushed past the wrapping and when sighting
the novelty jar, she giggled.

Put me & granddaddy in there when we fly away.

And her eight-track turned three chords
of the Chuck Wagon Gang "I Feel Like Traveling Home."
Her spin on the saying made me correct her

But it is a jar of your old lovers.

My one since I was fifteen. We are old lovers. Put us in there.

And so I did.

III
BBC Radio blaring, the windows rolled down in the rental,
I broadcasted their ashes like seed among
the hedgerows and field boundaries
of the A2 from Ballycastle to Carnlough.
Ann, Quay, Mary,
Cushendall, into the
very leaves of Ballypatrick Forest,
past the curious cows at
Watertop Farm on to
the sprinkled sheep of
the green Loughareema.
Another handful for the turf
of Squiress Dany Jain,
more for Tromra Road,
Tavnaghan Terrace, Mill Street—
fitting or our textiled ancestry.
The final flight for Glenariffe, Main,
Garron and Harbour.
They loved to hit the road.
Making miles was his business.
What would he have made of this strange terrain?
They are now part of the scenic route.
Littering the Glens of Antrim,
I quieten the radio
to sing Brumley's

Some glad morning when this life is over
I'll fly away. To a home on God's celestial shore.
I'll fly away.

Breaker, Diesel Smoke

A convoy of memories
Line up down the corridor
Revving up their engines for that last long haul—
The magic mile.

Bet you'd be happy to know
You won't have to ride in a bone box
You are already bedded.
Been horizontal for a while.

I wait for the 10-4.
Seems like the landline
Always sounds the sorry signal.

Come back
Come on
I put my face to yours
And say hello.
Hello?
Can you hear me?
Got a copy?
Can you see me?
Got your ears on?
Come back, Granddaddy.

When I ask
They only reply with how many
Candles you've got burning—
89.
He's declining.
Nervous system shutting down
Making him jerk.
Heavily medicated.
Eyes in "we gone" (on the by)
Head in the horizon.

Checking my eyelids for pinholes
I stand in the threshold
And rush back
Each time I see his mouth
Move. Silent ratchet-jaw, distant drone.
What's your 20?
Only his eyes shift when I say
His other half's name—Mary Lou.

Darktime
His black Velcro shoes
Opened and sitting on the window sill
Ready to go
Ground clouds
Follow the stripes home.

Forever eighty-eights.
Out, Pinky.

Molly Rice has held several residencies teaching poetry, storytelling, theatre, film, and English as a Second Language in hundreds of schools, colleges, and organizations in North Carolina, the United Kingdom, Ireland, Russia, and Hungary. She has taught for seventeen years at St. Stephens High School where she is director of the Tractor Shed Theatre. She is an award-winning theatre educator and her theatre program's civic engagement work with those who live on the margin has earned much praise. She has been published in various webzines and magazines including *Fortnight Magazine*, *The Stinging Fly*, *Iodine Poetry Journal*, and *Bloodshot: Journal of Contemporary Culture*. She was a contributor to a major anthology of poetry and art entitled, *A Conversation Piece: Poetry & Art*. She was published in *Voices and Vision: A Collection of Writings By and About Empowered Women*. Her chapbook *Mill Hill* was published by Finishing Line Press, Kentucky, in 2012. She resides with her husband and son, Adrian & Micah, in Hickory, North Carolina.

www.ingramcontent.com/pod-product-compliance
Lightning Source LLC
Chambersburg PA
CBHW021508090426
42739CB00007B/527